FINANCIALLY CARING FOR YOUR DISABLED CHILD

A GUIDE TO UNDERSTANDING THE MINNESOTA SUPPLEMENTAL NEEDS TRUST

By: Omni N. Kiecker, Esq.

FINANCIALLY CARING FOR YOUR DISABLED CHILD

A GUIDE TO UNDERSTANDING THE MINNESOTA SUPPLEMENTAL NEEDS TRUST

Disclaimer: This publication does not establish an attorney-client relationship. The contents of this book are not legal advice, they are for informational purposes only. This book is not a substitute for personalized legal advice. Consult a licensed attorney for professional legal advice. The author and publisher make no representations or warranties regarding the accuracy of this book.

Published by:

Bulldog Press LLC

Bulldog Press LLC
1005 Provence Ln
Belle Plaine, MN 56011

ISBN: 978-1-7338482-0-6 (Ebook)

ISBN: 978-1-7338482-1-3 (Paperback)

FINANCIALLY CARING FOR YOUR DISABLED CHILD

Introduction

You aren't reading this book for fun. You didn't pick it up because of the cover art and you didn't hear about it at a book club. You are reading this book because, like me, you heard the words, "Your child is disabled."

Disabled is a scary word that can mean many different things to many different people. I'm going to keep it simple. For the purposes of this book, a child is disabled if a medical professional has diagnosed him or her as disabled. It doesn't matter if the child has autism, epilepsy, paralysis or brain damage, the child is disabled.

You may have been told your child was disabled last week, last year, or even thirty years ago. The outcome doesn't change, however. What does change is you. You learn more about the disability, and you gain an understanding of how to best help your child learn, grow and succeed. You do this because you are the parent and it is part of your job. You know that you will always be there to take care of your child. You will be with them forever, taking care of their every need.

But what if that wasn't possible? What if something were to happen and you were injured, or an accident left you in a coma? What would happen to your disabled child? Who would take care of them? Who would protect them from social, financial, and sexual predators? If your child were to receive an inheritance from you, it is possible that your death could make your child a bigger target, which would affect their safety.

Why? Money. Predators seek out and take

advantage of people who are in a vulnerable situation. People search through obituaries looking for individuals who have died with the intention of deducing who may inherit money. They then attempt to scam the grieving loved ones. Having too much money can also disqualify someone from county and state resources. Your child may no longer qualify to receive aid and assistance from a social worker. Your child may no longer have a plan to help them decide what money should and shouldn't be spent on. Your child may no longer have a fiscal entity watching their budget. Your child could be alone.

I have gone through this. My son is extremely kind and caring. He wants to take care of people and if someone asked him for a thousand dollars, he would hand over a checkbook because he doesn't understand the value of money. He trusts that if someone calls, they really do need money for a relative, and that the person is in trouble. He trusts that the guy down the hall will pay him back. Sound familiar? Some of you, like me, have had to face the reality that your child is vulnerable.

If you do nothing and your child is a minor, you are in luck. The courts will intervene to appoint a guardian and a conservator. The courts will put your family to the test to decide who fits the best interests of the child. The money will then be limited and restricted and spent under the scrutiny of the court until the child turns 18, at which time, your child receives all remaining funds and they are legally alone over the age of majority, they are alone.

They have money to spend until it is stolen or spent down to a point where they can get back on state aid.

However, who is going to help them apply? Who can they go to for assistance with completing the paperwork? Do they know where their last tax returns are? Do they know what their medical expenses are? Do they know what help to ask for? Probably not. It took me months to navigate the Mn Choices Assessment System and all the paperwork to get my son help. I can't possibly imagine if he were to have to do it by himself. It would never get done and he would end up homeless.

I don't want that for my child, and I know that you don't want that for your child, either. No parent wants to see that for any of their children, disabled or otherwise. The good news is that the state of Minnesota recognizes the Supplemental Needs Trust. Great planning can prevent the worst nightmare from happening.

I'm writing this book so that you don't have to attempt to read Minnesota Statutes Chapter 524 that provides for what will happen to your estate when you die. I'm going to explain in plain English some parts of the statute that relate to disabled individuals and what can be done legally to assist them in retaining government benefits by using a Supplemental Needs Trust. Ultimately, the goal is that your disabled child will be able to get or stay on Medical Assistance for health care coverage. This will mean that you will have secured their financial future. And you will know that the Supplemental Needs Trust plan you put in place is legal and recognized as such by governmental institutions.

Throughout many sections, I am going to reference the statute and include language from the statute, but do not fear, good reader, I will always include a translation as to what the language means. I do this for two reasons:

1. I want to provide you with the authority for the information.

2. I want to stress the importance of hiring a lawyer to help with the creation of a Supplemental Needs Trust.

I would not attempt to rebuild my car engine because I am not a mechanic. Yes, I have YouTube, but I realize that the damage to my car could be significant. I would not attempt to fill my tooth or my husband's tooth because I am not dentist. I have a drill, but that does not mean I'm qualified to do the work of a trained professional. The same is true for creating legal documents. Yes, forms do exist online. Yes, any person can Google Supplemental Needs Trust and find many options. However, we all know, or we should know, that what the internet says is not always true. That is why I suggest that you use this book to inform and empower yourself about the Supplemental Needs Trust. Then, hire a lawyer who is well-versed in this area of the law, to properly create one to fit your needs.

This book is divided into different sections. Chapter one provides scenarios, including examples of the issues parents of special needs children face. Chapters two through five are about the law that you must first learn and understand before reading chapters six through ten, which apply the knowledge to explain the Supplemental Needs Trust. Chapters eleven and twelve provide additional financial considerations once the trust is established.

Chapter 1

Don't Let This be Your Child

The following scenarios illustrate some of the issues that disabled individuals may face when they lose their parents. They are examples of parents who have, with the best of intentions, attempted to do things right. However, when planning is not done properly, it can lead to some very sad circumstances.

Alone in a World

Mark is a single 45-year-old autistic man, who lives with his parents in the basement of their home. He drives to work and enjoys spending all his free time with his parents.

One day, while Mark was at work, both of his parents were killed in a car accident. Mark was extremely hurt by the loss of his parents but, being autistic, had no way of expressing his emotion and could not communicate his feelings. Mark's extended family wanted to make sure that he was doing well, but didn't have the capacity to take on an adult child. They were happy when Mark's nephew, Dippy, said he would move into the house to care for Mark. Dippy was never a good kid. Unfortunately, all of his bad habits became worse once he moved in with Mark. He would beat Mark for fun. He would make Mark buy drugs for him. He threatened to kill Mark's dog if Mark ever told. When Mark ran out of money to support Dippy, his dog was beaten to death and he was kicked out of the only home he had ever known. Mark now lives in a homeless shelter. He can't get a job because of the crimes he committed for Dippy. He has no money, no friends, and no dog.

Brother Doesn’t Ever Share

Mary’s mom, Angel, did everything right as a single mother of two. She did the very best she could on one income to take care of her children. But when she was diagnosed with stage 4 lung cancer, she knew that her daughter would be disqualified from Medical Assistance if she inherited anything. Therefore, Angel created a plan to disinherit her daughter. She put her house in her son’s name. She put her bank accounts in her son’s name and made him the beneficiary of her small employer-provided life insurance policy. When Angel died, her plan worked. Her son got everything. What Angel didn’t count on, and couldn’t have known, is that her son never planned to help or take care of his sister. He left the state with his new-found fortune and never returned again. Mary was left alone with no money, no family, and no understanding of what had just happened. Mary believed that her mom didn’t love her because she didn’t give her anything. Mary forever felt that she did something wrong because the mom who had always been there for her up until she died left her with nothing. And although Angel had thought she had made plans for Mary’s care, Mary received no help, no aid, and no assistance from her brother.

Hired the Wrong Attorney

Jan and Frank hired attorney Mr. Greasy. He was the well-known attorney around town that everyone used. After seeing his presentation, charts, and graphs, they were confident he was the right attorney to help them with estate planning that would ensure all four of their children were treated fairly. They wanted their oldest, Frank Jr., to get the farm. The twins, Max and Molly, were to each get large amounts of money equal to the value of the farm. Their disabled daughter, Daisy, was supposed to be taken care of by her siblings.

Attorney Greasy knew how to sell. He knew sales better than he knew the law. He sold Jan and Frank a trust. They paid a lot of money and felt confident that everything they needed was in the trust. Just to make sure, they went back every year to meet with Mr. Greasy. They paid for the meeting. They paid for updates. They paid for signing and they kept doing it because they cared about their children.

It wasn't until after Jan and Frank died that their children learned Attorney Mr. Greasy never funded the trust that he created for their parents. This meant they did not receive the assets in the method their parents had planned. Mr. Greasy never created any method to put anything into the trust, also known as "funding the trust". The trust was essentially an empty bucket.

There was no money, land, or assets titled into the name of the trust. Since there was no provision dealing with the farmland, it went through probate. All of Jan and Frank's possessions became public knowledge. Four children inherited the land and all the private property. Four children, including Daisy, inherited the life insurance, IRA, and pension fund. So, all siblings inherited equally. You may ask what is wrong with this scenario. Well, it is not what Jan and Frank wanted. Assuming all the kids get along, it will now take them time and money to work among themselves, to try to set in place the plan their parents had intended.

Poor Life Insurance Planning

James and Janet were hardworking parents. She worked as a secretary and he was a construction worker. They took good care of their two special needs kids and lived a simple life. Janet was struck by an illness that caused her to die. When James went to Janet's employer to collect her life insurance, he learned that she had only put both of her minor children down as the beneficiaries. James had to hire an attorney to get conservatorship of his own children so that he could collect the life insurance proceeds. James now must report to the court yearly on what he spends the funds on. It will be a yearly reminder that Janet should have named James as the primary beneficiary, and the trustee of the Supplemental Needs Trust as the alternate beneficiary It would have gone to an adult in the trustee capacity and they would not be required to report to the court yearly.

This is How You Do It!

Justin and Olivia were dedicated and loving parents who were proactive in taking steps to ensure their children would be provided for should anything happen to them. With the help of a knowledgeable investment advisor, they had life insurance and investments. They also structured a whole life policy on their son, Zander, before he was born, that they signed and paid for a month after his birth. They did the same for their second child, Mike, as well as their third, Genevieve. Justin and Olivia put money aside every month for their retirement and their children's insurance. They didn't go to Walt Disney World every year. They didn't take lavish tropical vacations. They certainly could have, but knew that they were making a wise decision to invest and save. After the birth of their third child, they drafted a will naming guardians for their children so that they would never become wards of the state. They also didn't want any relative orloved one to have to report to the court yearly regarding how the children's money was spent. They elected to select trustees in their will, rather than face a conservatorship. Paying to have a will drafted for them by an attorney was not cheap, but they didn't want to stake their children's lives on an online form. Their attorney also told them at the time of creation that they may need to update their plan from time to time, and advised them to review it every 3-5 years.

When Zander was 8, he was diagnosed with Attention Deficit Hyperactivity Disorder (ADHD) and Autism Spectrum Disorder (autism). The diagnosis turned the lives of Justin and Olivia upside down.

They had the perfect family with three wonderful, healthy children, and they were doing everything right in their minds to be good parents. They were confused. They wanted to learn as much as they could about the diagnosis and how to find help for their son. A teacher at Zander's school recommended that they contact the county for assistance. It seemed like a strange idea at first, but Justin and Oliva weren't going to turn down information. Olivia contacted the county, and was amazed by all the support they received. Zander qualified for Medical Assistance, and grant money. Justin and Olivia would no longer need to worry about co-pays or diapers for Zander. All tests, shots and appointments were either covered by their insurance or Medical Assistance (MA). The grant money was utilized for such things as modifying Zander's bike, purchasing a weighted blanket, and other necessary at-home medical supplies. Zander could go to a specialized day camp and attend HIPPO Therapy sessions that his parents could otherwise not afford. Zander's parents could also pay others to help him get to and from his weekly therapy sessions.

Post diagnosis, Zander's parents began to wonder, what if something happened to them? Would the guardian they chose for their children when they were babies still be willing to care for Zander with all of his current medical needs? Would their life insurance be enough to take care of Zander in life? Would Zander be able to manage money in the future or would he be a victim of theft? Would Zander still be able to attend all of his therapy sessions and have all his needs met the way that they could?

The chosen guardians for Zander and his siblings assured Justin and Olivia that they would absolutely care for all children, no matter their abilities or disabilities. The chosen trustees said that they would absolutely take care of money for Zander and his siblings until they each reached the age of thirty, the age selected in their will.

Justin and Olivia ran into an issue, though. When they asked Zander's county case worker what would happen to Zander if something happened to them, they were told that Zander's eligibility for services would become income-based. If Zander inherited his parents' life insurance, that would disqualify him from help. He would no longer receive MA, meaning his inheritance would be spent on insurance, co-pays, and therapy. Little would be left for him to enjoy the wayhis parents wanted him to.

Olivia had a good friend that suggested she contact the attorney that drafted her will. It had been some time since they had it reviewed, so she called and made an appointment. When reviewing their documents, Justin and Olivia's attorney discussed Zander's disability and the issues he would face if he ever had money in his name. The attorney told them that she had a tool that could help with just that issue – a Supplemental Needs Trust. The trust would cost more than their original will and they would have to modify their current plan, but it would ensure that Zander could continue to receive aid and assistance from the state while being able to enjoy the benefits of an inheritance.

The chart on the next few pages explains the very basic different potential outcomes for any special needs child based on their parents' level of planning.

*Every disabled child is different. If they are able to earn an income, that puts them above the county base limits on their own. They will not be eligible for additional aid, even if they have a trust.

	NO PLAN	WILL	SUPPLEMENTAL NEEDS TRUST
RESIDENCE	Ward of the state	Moves in with Guardian until 18	Moves in with Guardian permanently
MONEY	Conservatorship	Trustee manages money	Trustee manages money
REMAINDER	Remainder at age 18	Remainder at age parents chose	No control over money
CONTROL OF ESTATE	Executor must be appointed	Personal representative of estate	Trustee for trust
DISPOSITION OF ESTATE	Probate	Probate	Probate

INSURANCE	Abandoned by state insurance at age 18	Abandoned by state insurance at age 18	State Medical Assistance support*
COUNTY ASSISTANCE	Spend down to get assistance	Spend down to get assistance	No spend down
HOUSING	No Housing support after 18	No Housing Support after 18	Housing penalty unless ABLE account
FISCALLY VULNERABLE	Financially vulnerable	Financially vulnerable	Financially secure
PLANNING TIME	Easy	Time-consuming	Significant planning
FINAL DISPOSITION	Alone	Alone	Support for life
COST	No cost to parents	Some cost to parents	Greater cost to parents

Chapter 2

Guardianship

All your legal options are based on “The Law.” We need to know and understand the law before we can apply the law. This chapter is designed to do just that. Follow along as I explain various sections of the MN Statute and what they mean. This is what your friends and family members would have to go through to gain physical custody of your children.

The verbiage from the statute will be in *italics.*

<u>Guardianship</u> - Minnesota Statue 524.5-313.

(a) *A guardian shall be subject to the control and direction of the court at all times and in all things.*

A guardian is going to be physically in charge of, or in control of, the physical person of a disabled individual. The court will always be in charge of the guardian.

(b) *The court shall grant to a guardian only those powers necessary to provide for the demonstrated needs of the ward.*

Just because you select a guardian for your child, once they become an adult, the state wants them to be able to operate without someone physically in control of them.
Therefore, the judge has many standard options to choose from.

(c) *The court may appoint a guardian if it determines that all the powers and duties listed in this section are needed to provide for the needs of the incapacitated person. The court may also appoint a guardian if it determines that a guardian is needed to provide for the needs of the incapacitated person through the exercise of some, but not all, of the powers and duties listed in this section. The duties and powers of a guardian or those which the court may grant to a guardian include, but are not limited to:*

This is at the very top of the guardianship application. For the purposes of the application, the incapacitated person is your child.

(1) the power to have custody of the ward and the power to establish a place of abode within or outside the state, except as otherwise provided in this clause. The ward or any interested person may petition the court to prevent or to initiate a change in abode. A ward may not be admitted to a regional treatment center by the guardian except:

(i) after a hearing under chapter 253B;
(ii) for outpatient services; or
(iii) for the purpose of receiving temporary care for a specific period of time not to exceed 90 days in any calendar year;

The guardian can name where your child lives. Your child can ask for their place of residence to be changed and they can't be put into treatment without a court order.

(2) the duty to provide for the ward's care, comfort, and maintenance needs, including food, clothing, shelter, health care, social and

recreational requirements, and, whenever appropriate, training, education, and habilitation or rehabilitation. The guardian has no duty to pay for these requirements out of personal funds. Whenever possible and appropriate, the guardian should meet these requirements through governmental benefits or services to which the ward is entitled, rather than from the ward's estate. Failure to satisfy the needs and requirements of this clause shall be grounds for removal of a private guardian, but the guardian shall have no personal or monetary liability;

The guardian is in charge of the care of your child. Food, clothing, and education are some of the categories, meaning they will purchase groceries for your child, buy them appropriate clothes, and make sure that they can get to and from school.

Notice that the guardian is not supposed to use their own funds, but government funds that your child is entitled to. For the purposes of a Supplemental Needs Trust, this is extremely important. If the child has too much money, there may not be as much funding of governmental benefits. Your child's inheritance could be spent on transportation if they don't have a Supplemental Needs Trust protecting it.

(3) *the duty to take reasonable care of the ward's clothing, furniture, vehicles, and other personal effects, and, if other property requires protection, the power to seek appointment of a conservator of the estate. The guardian must give notice by mail to interested persons prior to the disposition of the ward's clothing, furniture,*

vehicles, or other personal effects. The notice must inform the person of the right to object to the disposition of the property within ten days of the date of mailing and to petition the court for a review of the guardian's proposed actions. Notice of the objection must be served by mail or personal service on the guardian and the ward unless the ward is the objector. The guardian served with notice of an objection to the disposition of the property may not dispose of the property unless the court approves the disposition after a hearing;

The guardian must take care of your child's possessions. This includes valuables, guns, and heirlooms you leave for your children. They are in charge of protecting items such as these for your child.

(4) (i) the power to give any necessary consent to enable the ward to receive necessary medical or other professional care, counsel, treatment, or service, except that no guardian may give consent for psychosurgery, electroshock, sterilization, or experimental treatment of any kind unless the procedure is first approved by order of the court as provided in this clause. The guardian shall not consent to any medical care for the ward which violates the known conscientious, religious, or moral belief of the ward;

(ii) a guardian who believes a procedure described in item (i) requiring prior court approval to be necessary for the proper care of the ward, shall petition the court for an order and, in the case of a public guardianship under chapter 252A, obtain the written recommendation of the commissioner of human services. The court shall fix the time and place for the hearing and shall give notice to the ward in such manner as specified in section 524.5-308 and to interested persons. The court shall appoint an attorney to represent the ward who is not represented by counsel, provided that such appointment shall expire upon the expiration of the appeal time for the order issued by the court under this section or the order dismissing a petition, or upon such other time or event as the court may direct. In every case the court shall determine if the procedure is in the best interest of the ward. In making its determination, the court shall consider a written medical report which specifically considers the medical risks of the procedure, whether alternative, less restrictive methods of treatment could be used to protect the best interest of the ward, and any recommendation of the commissioner of human services for a public ward. The standard of proof is that of clear and convincing evidence;

(iii) in the case of a petition for sterilization of a developmentally disabled ward, the court shall appoint a licensed physician, a psychologist who is qualified in the diagnosis and treatment of developmental disability, and a social worker

who is familiar with the ward's social history and adjustment or the case manager for the ward to examine or evaluate the ward and to provide written reports to the court. The reports shall indicate why sterilization is being proposed, whether sterilization is necessary and is the least intrusive method for alleviating the problem presented, and whether it is in the best interest of the ward. The medical report shall specifically consider the medical risks of sterilization, the consequences of not performing the sterilization, and whether alternative methods of contraception could be used to protect the best interest of the ward;

(iv) any ward whose right to consent to a sterilization has not been restricted under this section or section 252A.101 may be sterilized only if the ward consents in writing or there is a sworn acknowledgment by an interested person of a nonwritten consent by the ward. The consent must certify that the ward has received a full explanation from a physician or registered nurse of the nature and irreversible consequences of the sterilization;

(v) a guardian or the public guardian's designee who acts within the scope of authority conferred by letters of guardianship under section 252A.101, subdivision 7, and according to the standards established in this chapter or in chapter 252A shall not be civilly or criminally liable for the provision of any necessary medical care, including, but not limited to, the administration of psychotropic medication or the

implementation of aversive and deprivation procedures to which the guardian or the public guardian's designee has consented;

The guardian is in charge of and responsible for your child's medical care.

(5) in the event there is no duly appointed conservator of the ward's estate, the guardian shall have the power to approve or withhold approval of any contract, except for necessities, which the ward may make or wish to make;

The guardian can prevent your child from entering into a contract, even if it' something as simple as signing an unwanted magazine subscription.

(6) the duty and power to exercise supervisory authority over the ward in a manner which limits civil rights and restricts personal freedom only to the extent necessary to provide needed care and services;

The guardian can put a tracker on your child to know where they are, in order to better provide for their care.

(7) if there is no acting conservator of the estate for the ward, the guardian has the power to apply on behalf of the ward for any assistance, services, or benefits available to the ward through any unit of government;

The guardian can apply for government money for your child if the conservator is not already doing so. Notice a pattern that the guardian should apply for state aid. The guardian cannot spend money that would affect state aid and the guardian can't spend their own money.

(8) unless otherwise ordered by the court, the ward retains the right to vote.

Your child has the right to vote when they turn 18.

In summary, if you die and have a minor child, the child will live with their other parent if he/she is still alive and fit to parent. If both parents are dead, and you have not appointed a guardian for your child in an estate planning document, then the court can appoint a guardian for your child. The job of the guardian is like that of a parent, but they don't have to use their money to pay for the child's needs. In some instances, they can even get paid to care for your child. This guardianship ends when the child is no longer a minor.

Once a child reaches the age of majority, someone needs to be appointed as guardian to make decisions on behalf of the disabled child, even if the child is still living with their parents.

A properly drafted Supplemental Needs Trust allows for parents to appoint a guardian who can care for their disabled child at any age. Minor or adult, the care of the child will be continuous by the person you choose.

Chapter 3

Conservatorship

To simplify the legal concept, conservatorship means to be in charge of another's finances. If you have a properly drafted Supplemental Needs Trust, you can choose the conservator for your child if you were to pass away. The statutory language below outlines what would happen and who would be selected if you did not select a conservator.

Once again, the verbiage from the statue will be in *italics*.

Conservatorship. Minnesota Statue 524.5-

413.

(1) *a conservator, guardian of the estate, or other like fiduciary appointed or recognized by an appropriate court of any other jurisdiction in which the protected person resides;*

(2) *a person nominated as conservator by the respondent, including the respondent's most recent nomination made in a durable power of attorney, if the respondent has attained 14 years of age and at the time of the nomination had sufficient capacity to express a preference;*

(3) *an agent appointed by the respondent to*

manage the respondent's property under a durable power of attorney;

(4) *the spouse of the respondent;*

(5) *an adult child of the respondent;*

(6) *a parent of the respondent;*

(7) *an adult with whom the respondent has resided for more than six months before the filing of the petition;*

(8) *an adult who is related to the respondent by blood, adoption, or marriage; and*

(9) *any other adult or a professional conservator.*

Will or no will, once your child reaches the age of majority, they are legally on their own with their inheritance, unless you created a trust that says otherwise.

Chapter 4

Legal Options
Supplemental Needs Trust

All your legal options are based on "The Law." We need to know and understand the law before we can apply the law. This chapter is designed to do just that. Follow along as I explain various sections of the MN Statute and what they mean.

The verbiage from the statue will be in *italics*.

<u>Supplemental Needs Trust</u> – Minnesota Statue 501C.1205

> *(a) Except as allowed by subdivision 2 or 3, a provision in a trust that provides for the suspension, termination, limitation, or diversion of the principal, income, or beneficial interest of a beneficiary if the beneficiary applies for, is determined eligible for, or receives public assistance or benefits under a public health care program is unenforceable as against the public policy of this state, without regard to the irrevocability of the trust or the purpose for which the trust was created.*

No other type of trust can do what a Supplemental Needs Trust does.

> *(b) This subdivision applies to trust provisions created after July 1, 1992. For purposes of this section, a trust provision is created on the date of execution of the first instrument that contains the provision, even though the trust provision is later amended or reformed or the trust is not funded until a later date.*

If you are reading this book and considering writing a Supplemental Needs Trust, paragraph (b) doesn't apply to you, as it is after 1992. If you have a Supplemental Needs Trust that was created before 1992, see a lawyer for assistance.

Subd. 2. Supplemental trusts for persons with disabilities.

This must be a medically recorded disability. The person does not need to be on medication for the disability, but it must be in their medical record that a medical doctor has declared them disabled. See an attorney if you want more information as to whether the disability you are concerned about meets the qualifications for a Supplemental Needs Trust.

(a) It is the public policy of this state to enforce Supplemental Needs Trusts as provided in this subdivision.

If you have a Supplemental Needs Trust, other institutions must recognize it and honor it.

(b) For purposes of this subdivision, a "Supplemental Needs Trust" is a trust created for the benefit of a person with a disability and funded by someone other than the trust beneficiary, the beneficiary's spouse, or anyone obligated to pay any sum for damages or any other purpose to or for the benefit of the trust beneficiary under the terms of a settlement agreement or judgment.

This trust cannot be funded by your disabled child, their spouse, or anyone owing money to the disabled child. This would include money received from such things as a settlement from a car accident, or medical malpractice lawsuit money. It must be funded by someone else – parent, sibling, child, long-distance relative, clergy, the options are endless.

> *(c) For purposes of this subdivision, a "person with a disability" means a person who, prior to creation of a trust which otherwise qualifies as a Supplemental Needs Trust for the person's benefit:*

This is the definition of a person with a disability in minute detail.

> *(1) is considered to be a person with a disability under the disability criteria specified in title II or title XVI of the Social Security Act; or*

As if attempting to read the statute isn't enough, they direct the reader to look to another source.

> *(2) has a physical or mental illness or condition which, in the expected natural course of the illness or condition, either prior to or following creation of the trust, to a reasonable degree of medical certainty, is expected to:*
> *(i) last for a continuous period of 12 months or more; and*
> *(ii)substantially impair the person's ability to provide for the person's care or custody.*

It must be a disability that will last more than a year. It cannot be a broken leg that will heal in a few months.

Disability may be established conclusively for purposes of this subdivision by the written opinion of a licensed professional who is qualified to diagnose the illness or condition, confirmed by the written opinion of a second licensed professional who is qualified to diagnose the illness or condition.

As I said earlier, it is best to have it in writing by a doctor that a person is disabled.

(d) The general purpose of a Supplemental Needs Trust must be to provide for the reasonable living expenses and other basic needs of a person with a disability when benefits from publicly funded benefit programs are not sufficient to provide adequately for those needs. Subject to the restrictions contained in this paragraph, a Supplemental Needs Trust may authorize distributions to provide for all or any portion of the reasonable living expenses of the beneficiary. A Supplemental Needs Trust may allow or require distributions only in ways and for purposes that supplement or complement the benefits available under medical assistance, Minnesota supplemental aid, and other publicly funded benefit programs for disabled persons. A Supplemental Needs Trust must contain provisions that prohibit disbursements that would have the effect of replacing, reducing, or substituting for publicly funded benefits otherwise available to the beneficiary or rendering the beneficiary ineligible for publicly funded benefits.

The last sentence is <u>very important</u> in that the Supplemental Needs Trust cannot pay out any funds that publicly funded programs or other funds will pay for. The trust can't make the person unable to get money from other sources. This is the key to everything a parent is trying to accomplish by creating a Supplemental Needs Trust for their child. If the child has an expense related to the disability, the publicly funded organization should pay first. It is only if it is found that the organization cannot meet those needs that the trust can supplement, so that the disabled individual is assisted.

> *(e) A Supplemental Needs Trust is not enforceable if the trust beneficiary becomes a patient or resident after age 64 in a state institution or nursing facility for six months or more and, due to the beneficiary's medical need for care in an institutional setting, there is no reasonable expectation that the beneficiary will ever be discharged from the institution or facility. For purposes of this paragraph "reasonable expectation" means that the beneficiary's attending physician has certified that the expectation is reasonable. For purposes of this paragraph, a beneficiary participating in a group residential program is not deemed to be a patient or resident in a state institution or nursing facility.*

If the person is expected to be in a nursing home for six months or more, the nursing home can look to the trust money to help pay for their care.

> *(f) The trust income and assets of a Supplemental Needs Trust are considered available to the beneficiary for medical assistance purposes to the*

extent they are considered available to the beneficiary under medical assistance, Supplemental Security Income, or Minnesota family investment program methodology, whichever is used to determine the beneficiary's eligibility for medical assistance. For other public assistance programs established or administered under state law, assets and income will be considered available to the beneficiary in accordance with the methodology applicable to the program.

Do not allow the beneficiary to have access to the income or assets of the trust. Do not allow the beneficiary to have control of the trust.

(g) Nothing in this subdivision requires submission of a Supplemental Needs Trust to a court for interpretation or enforcement.

The court doesn't want to try to interpret the language of the trust. It is written by lawyers to work and the court trusts them.

(h) Paragraphs (a) to (g) apply to Supplemental Needs Trusts whenever created, but the limitations and restrictions in paragraphs (c) to (g) apply only to trusts created after June 30, 1993.

Again, if you are reading this book and thinking about creating a Supplemental Needs Trust, don't worry. It is after 1993. If you have a trust that was created before 1993, see a lawyer.

Subd. 3.Supplemental Needs Trusts under federal law.

A trust created on or after August 11, 1993, which qualifies as a Supplemental Needs Trust for a person with a disability under United States Code, title 42, section 1396p(c)(2)(B)(iv) or 1396p(d), as amended by section 13611(b) of the Omnibus Budget Reconciliation Act of 1993, Public Law 103-66, commonly known as OBRA 1993, is enforceable, and the courts of this state may authorize creation and funding of a trust which so qualifies.

If you have a trust that was drafted properly by a lawyer who understands Supplemental Needs Trusts, you don't need to worry about a conflict with federal law.

Subd. 4.Annual filing requirement for Supplemental Needs Trusts.
(a) A trustee of a trust under subdivision 3 and United States Code, title 42, section 1396p(d)(4)(A) or (C), shall submit to the commissioner of human services, at the time of a beneficiary's request for medical assistance, the following information about the trust:
(1) a copy of the trust instrument; and

(2) an inventory of the beneficiary's trust account assets and the value of those assets.

If the person the trust was created for applies for Medical Assistance, the trustee needs to give the commissioner of human services (government) a copy of the trust.

(b) *A trustee of a trust under subdivision 3 and United States Code, title 42, section 1396p(d)(4)(A) or (C), shall submit an accounting of the beneficiary's trust account to the commissioner of human services at least annually until the trust, or the beneficiary's interest in the trust, terminates. Accountings are due on the anniversary of the execution date of the trust unless another annual date is established by the terms of the trust. The accounting must include the following information for the accounting period:*

(1) an inventory of trust assets and the value of those assets at the beginning of the accounting period;

(2) additions to the trust during the accounting period and the source of those additions;

(3) itemized distributions from the trust during the accounting period, including the purpose of the distributions and to whom the distributions were made;

If the person who the trust was created for is on Medical Assistance, the trustee must provide yearly information to the government.

Chapter 5

Additional Legislation

Federal Legislation

The Patient Protection and Affordable Care Act (PPACA), also known as the Affordable Care Act (ACA), and often referred to simply as Obamacare, is a United States Federal Statute signed into law by President Barack Obama in 2010.

The act kept the existing structure of Medicare, Medicaid, and the employer market, but individual markets were radically overhauled. Insurers in these markets are made to accept all applicants and charge the same rates, regardless of pre-existing conditions or sex.

One of the goals of the act was to make it possible for everyone in the United States to have health insurance. If a disabled individual applies for a job, they cannot be denied health insurance coverage because of the disability. If they have expenses, their individual insurance will pay first, then other government programs such as Medical Assistance. It is only after those programs have paid medical expenses that the Supplemental Needs Trust can pay for medical needs.

Medicare is a national health insurance program. It provides health insurance to adults age 65 and older. It also provides health insurance to younger people with certain disabilities. Covered disabilities are determined by the Social Security Administration. If your child is on Medicare, it is possible that an inheritance could disqualify them from receiving assistance.

State Legislation

Medicaid, also known as Medical Assistance, or MA, is a state managed insurance program for people age 64 or older. It also covers younger persons with disabilities who have an income at or below 138% of the Federal Poverty Level.

More information about the Minnesota Department of Human Resources Income and Eligibility guidelines for the state health care programs can be found online. Please note that the purpose of this book is not about how to get someone qualified to be on these programs. This book is about protecting the disabled who already qualify for these programs so they may continue receiving aid after receiving an inheritance, and assisting them in managing their money when they turn 18.

Simply put, if parents leave money to a disabled child on medical assistance, the gift will disqualify the child from Medical Assistance until the money is used up. It doesn't matter how young or old the child is.

Chapter 6

The Protected Child

The protected child, also known as the ward, is under the protection of the court because they are a minor or disabled. If parents or legal guardians pass away and a child is under the age of 18, they may become a ward of the state of Minnesota. If legal guardians of a disabled individual, regardless of age, pass away, they may become a ward of the state of Minnesota. Having a good estate plan can help prevent this.

The Disabled Child

Parents of minors on Medical Assistance in Minnesota know that it is not an easy task to get them qualified for assistance. The paperwork is extensive and the time it takes to gather and submit everything is exhausting.

Not everyone is guaranteed Medical Assistance because it is a needs-based program. A minor child must qualify every year. What if that child should suddenly inherit wealth? If they receive a gift or inheritance of cash from someone directly to them, there is a good chance they would become ineligible for Medical Assistance. In theory, this would be okay because they could financially pay for the care they need. However, just because they can financially afford to pay for the care does not mean that they can mentally handle budgeting and paying for the care. Special needs children and adults tend to have a lot of medical bills. It can be extremely difficult for a parent to take care of the child and stay current on all the paperwork and bills.

It doesn't have to be the parents dying that could disqualify a child. It could be any influx of money or assets from any source. If a non-profit gives the family the gift of a modified vehicle to allow them to more easily transport the child, it could disqualify them. If a church or charity creates a fundraiser for the disabled individual, it could disqualify them.

Now imagine if both parents passed away and left a special needs minor child. This can and does happen. Imagine your child struggling to cope with the loss of parents. Imagine your family trying to juggle to figure out care for your child. Imagine the county interfering with your child's life by attempting to establish a place of residence that isn't with a relative – possibly even foster care. Yikes! The good news is that by properly drafting a Supplemental Needs Trust, those worries can be put to rest.

Imagine if both parents pass away and leave a special needs adult child. This can and does happen. A lot of my older clients are concerned about this. Their child has lived with them their whole lives. They are everything to their 60-year-old child, but they know they won't live forever. Imagine the county interfering with your child's life by attempting to establish a place of residence, possibly a group home. Again, yikes! As explained above with minors, a Supplemental Needs Trust can also relieve these worries by preventing these scary scenarios.

Chapter 7

Selecting the Guardian

The best way to explain the role of a guardian is to determine who the child or disabled adult should live with. Who is going to be physically in charge of helping them with their day-to-day needs or getting them the care they need on a daily basis?

For a disabled adult, the parents should consider other loved ones who could take the child into their home. They may also want to visit group homes that might be a good fit for their child.

For a disabled child, I suggest that you consider other loved ones who are close with the individual. This might be a grandparent, aunt, or even older cousin. Look for the person in your lives who will best raise the child in the same way you would if you could do it yourself. Look for the values and qualities in that person that you feel are important. Honesty, respect, faith, family. Whatever it is that you value and want your child to value. Name someone who also has those qualities.

I also suggest that you might want to have a conversation with the person before naming them as a potential future guardian of your child. Ask them how they feel about your child. How would they feel about bringing a disabled child into their home? Would they be comfortable working with your child and their needs daily? Remind them that now is the time to be honest. If they have reservations, it is better that they say so now. It's not because they don't love your child, they just may not be equipped to raise them.

For them to make an informed decision, you also need to be honest about your child and their disability. How much care do they need daily? What are their strengths and weaknesses? What does their schedule look like? Be honest about what you could be signing them up for. If you hide anything for fear that it would make someone not want to care for your child, you are setting the caregiver up for a situation they might not have bargained for, and in truth, might not be equipped to handle. These situations never go well for the child.

Caution: Do NOT automatically assume the relative who has the most money should be named as guardian of your children. We all know that money does not equal happiness, but many parents still do just this. Money does not tell you anything about a person's wealth.

Also, of note, is that some people living with disabilities will always need a guardian in their life, or someone to help take care of their activities of daily living. If your child fits into this category, it is especially important that you look across generations when naming guardians. If you are a young parent and have a young child, you may look to your parents as alternate guardians. However, it is important to consider how old your parents will be when your child is twenty. Would they still be able to provide the level of care your child needs? If not, that is okay. You can still name your parents as primary guardian and then name someone else, such as a sibling as alternate guardian.

Chapter 8

Selecting the Trustee

A Supplemental Needs Trust cannot be funded by the disabled child or with their funds. It can, however, be started and funded by the parents. I typically suggest that the parents of the special needs child be the original trustees of the trust. This is because they are most closely tied to the child and, other than the child, they have the most to lose if the trust is mismanaged. The parents also know the child. They know the wants and needs of their children, even if they are non-verbal.

I also suggest that parents name one or more successor trustees in case they are unable to someday take care of the child's funds. This could be through death or a disability like Alzheimer's or dementia.

When considering who should be a successor trustee, know that you can name one or more people, or in some cases, a financial institution. I say "in some cases" because larger bank and trust companies have minimum deposit limits. They do this because they need to be able to make money from managing the trust funds. I suggest that if you are interested in an organization, you consult with them, and ask what their requirements are. Some organizations in Minnesota run Pot Trusts for individuals where the funds from many individuals are combined into a structure that is managed similar to that of a large individual trust. If you like the idea of having corporate oversight rather than individual choice, this might be an option for you.

What if you don't qualify for a bank and trust company, or you simply don't want the possibility of an organization managing your child's money if you can't as trustee? Then what? Some people turn to their family next. Some additional options are listed on the next page.

Remember that many people don't understand the role of a trustee when asked to be one. Remind them that it is the child's money that they will be caring for, not your actual child.

Your Parents

They might be a good choice if they are good with money. However, they age as your child does. How old will they be when you child is 20? 40? 60?

Your Siblings

Where are they in their life? What could be changing in their life? Are they good with money? If they can't pay their rent, I would suggest you consider someone else.

Your Friends

How well do you know your friends? How close are you with them? How might their lives change? I suggest that you talk to the friend first.

Your Financial Advisor

This is someone in your life that you know is good with money. You have hired them to manage your money. Why not have them mange your child's if something happens to you? I strongly encourage you to speak with them before you name them. What if they were no longer with that company? Would you still trust them? Jane Doe as an advisor for XYZ Company? Jane Doe as a cashier?

Your Accountant

See Financial Advisor.

Your Lawyer

This can be tricky. This could be unethical and get the attorney disbarred if not done correctly. Another family member, who thought they would make a wonderful trustee, may wonder why they were not selected for the position. This could cause them to investigate who is in charge. When they find out that the same person that drafted the document is now also in charge of the money, they could allege misconduct on behalf of the attorney. They could claim that the attorney only drafted themselves into the document to benefit financially. Even though the claim is not true, allegations of misconduct are bad for an attorney.

Chapter 9

Where to Begin

Now that you know about what a Supplemental Needs Trust can do and what roles are involved, where you do begin? How do you decide if a Supplemental Needs Trust is right for your child and your family? I will admit that as an attorney with a disabled child, I feel that a Supplemental Needs Trust is a wonderful tool for all families with disabled children. Here are some things to consider if one is right for you.

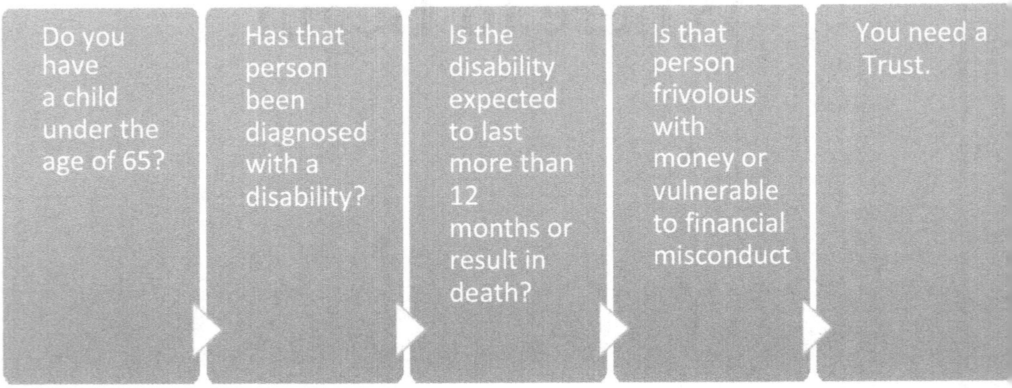

Age is an easy factor to qualify. Either you are under the age of 65 or not. A disability diagnosis is more difficult Typically, people with blindness, mental illness, Down syndrome, or brain damage are considered disabled. But that is not a complete list. Again, the best person to speak to about your child is their primary care doctor. They may refer you to a specialist for additional testing. Parents, I encourage you not to give up. If you have a gut feeling that something isn't right, trust your gut and seek answers. Some conditions such as autism are not always easily identifiable and may not be diagnosed until later in life, such as 8-10 years old. Some children are so good at learning to adapt or modify their learning or daily tasks that it isn't noticed until they are more involved in a social setting.

After your child is diagnosed as disabled, I encourage your family to have a team meeting. If the child is young and unable to understand the conversation, they need not take part. I encourage you to bring in everyone who plays a role in the disabled person's life. Some say to have a family meeting where only the immediate relatives meet to talk about/with the disabled person. While this may be necessary later, I also encourage you to involve a broader circle of people. Family may not be with the person during all waking hours. They may not know or see the needs of the person daily if they only see them at breakfast and suppertime. Consider who this might be in your life.

- Parents
- Grandparents
- Caregivers
- Co-workers
- Teachers
- Children

When meeting with this group, be open and honest. If the disabled person is present, don't talk about him or her as if they aren't there. You all care about the disabled person and want the best for them. Sometimes that means truly opening your eyes to their disabilities and their handicaps. Are they vulnerable to abuse? Are they able to manage money? Would they be okay navigating the world alone without someone assisting them in managing their assets and income?

If the person is young, it may be difficult to answer these questions, but try your best. The future gets fuzzier the more you extrapolate the possibilities. Some may think the best of the future and that there will be a cure. Others may think the worst. That is why multiple viewpoints are needed for balance. Ultimately, it will be the relatives closest to the person that make the final decision, but the input of everyone is valuable for consideration.

Where is the person at in life? Where do you see them in 5 or 10 years? What are your goals for the person? Are they capable of attaining them in time? Are they financially capable of attaining them? Would they be able to attain them without support? Match those goals to what is currently available for support. Is that enough? Would it help if there was another person to assist in managing the money?

As parents, it was hard for my husband and me to accept that our son was disabled. We knew that he was different and that there was always something that made him special and not like other children. He was the hidden child that was so good at finding ways to adapt that he was not diagnosed until he was nine years old, a direct result of being put into more social situations in his school. At that time, we had a meeting. For us, it was my husband and me, along with my child's teachers and pediatrician. As parents, we learned that everyone recognized that something was special. The public school had already tested him and declared him normal. They said he had an IQ of 72, so he was not clinically cognitively delayed, he was just a slower learner than his peers. However, because he had developed coping mechanisms and was able to make eye contact, he tested well on the other tests and "performed beyond his abilities," there was nothing they would do to help him. WOW! That was a smack in the face. I cried for days. Luckily his teachers, pediatrician and parents knew the diagnosis was WRONG! We went to Fraser, a professional autism center in Minnesota for testing. They spent weeks testing my son. Unlike the public school, they did not do a test, grade it, and jump to a conclusion. They put my son through a variety of tests over many weeks. They then took time to analyze the results, and as medical professionals, diagnose my son. Do you see how the team helped to make the difference? As parents, if we had relied solely on testing from the public school's special education department, we might have just taken the answer, put our son in Special Education Classroom, and continued. But, as a team, we triumphed for my son. Working with Fraser allowed us to establish a more specialized course of action and keep my son out of special education.

Chapter 10

Hiring an Attorney

You have decided that a Supplemental Needs Trust is right for your loved one. Now what? Where do you begin? You can't simply go to the store and buy a Supplemental Needs Trust. You cannot have a Supplemental Needs Trust shipped to you by Amazon. Believe me, I checked. So where do you start? At this point in the book you are excited. You know that there is a very valuable legal tool available to help protect the assets of the disabled, but you can't find it. I've read the reviews of other books where they claim that the authors combine material from Google searches and leave them hanging.

I also warn you that just doing an internet search for a Supplemental Needs Trust Attorney will bring up the names of attorneys who have hired good advertisers and marketers. I know because I've had the opportunity to read a document that was drafted by another attorney with the title Supplemental Needs Trust. However, in reading the language of the trust, the title was the only thing that was even remotely related to what a Supplemental Needs Trust should be. It was a standard trust with a different label the attorney charged more for, claiming it provided additional protection. This was not the consequence the parents intended.

Before you hire someone, I suggest you start by exploring all your options. Yes, you can do an internet search. You can also ask the social services agencies that you are connected with if they suggest someone. Ask your friends and neighbors. Talk to people.

A great referral is better than a blind internet search any day. I am not a doctor. However, if someone asked me for the name of a good one, I'd be happy to help.

Call everyone. Take notes and compare. Ask questions. If someone can't talk to you without an appointment, are they going to be too busy for you once you are a client? If someone can't answer a question off the cuff about a Supplemental Needs Trust, are they the best choice when considering an attorney who specializes in that area? I'm not telling you to take a bunch of time. Be courteous and professional. Ask the attorney if they have a few minutes to answer a couple questions. Explain that you are trying to find an attorney who might best fit your needs for setting up a Supplemental Needs Trust. I will tell you that the attorney will say that they cannot give you legal advice. This IS NOT blowing you off. This is them being responsible for professional liability reasons. Like a good job interview, have your questions prepared in advance.

Some examples might include:

How many Supplemental Needs Trusts have you drafted?

What is your experience working with the disabled?

What do you know about disability benefits?

Would you recommend that the disabled individual be the trustee? Trick Question: If they say yes, hang up.

What else do you do in addition to Supplemental Needs Trusts?

What types of continuing legal education have you participated in?

What types of continuing legal education have you instructed?

How long does the process take?

Who will be drafting the document, an attorney or a paralegal?

Can I take the disabled person's bank account and just turn it into a trust? Trick Question: The answer is no.

These are all questions you can ask on the phone before ever meeting with an attorney. Once you have decided on a few people that you feel are a right fit, schedule a time to meet with them. When meeting with the attorney, how do they make you feel?

- Was it easy to get an appointment with them?

- Was the appointment time convenient for you?

- Was the attorney willing to meet with you in your home so that you didn't have to travel or find a sitter for your child or special needs adult?

- Was the attorney comfortable with the special needs person?

- Did the attorney seem knowledgeable about the lives of a family with a special needs relative?

Beyond the gut feeling about the attorney, did they seem knowledgeable about the area of law? The following are some questions that you can ask to help you determine if they are.

1. Is there an age limit for a Supplemental Needs Trust in Minnesota?

   Yes

2. Is a Minnesota Supplemental Needs Trust good in other States?

   No, but it could be honored by them. It is best to get a new trust if you move to another state.

3. Do I have to give a bank a copy of the trust?

   No, they don't need the full Supplemental Needs Trust A Certificate of Trust will do for their purposes.

4. Does the trust have to be updated?

   Like other legal documents, it is recommended it be reviewed every 3-5 years or when major life changes happen.

5. Can the trust funds be used to pay for housing?

   NO!!!! That is one of the biggest mistakes unqualified lawyers tell people. If you use the trust to pay for housing, there could be a deduction in state funds.

You have vetted the attorney by phone. You have spoken to them in person. During that initial consultation, which is hopefully free, be sure to ask for a copy of the retainer agreement and fee structure. Do not sign it if you don't feel comfortable. Consider the cost carefully, however. Even if you feel comfortable with the attorney, if the fees are out of your price range, you don't want to end up hiring an attorney you ultimately can't afford.

Also, make sure that you know the process the attorney follows when working with clients. Do they have a paralegal do an intake, after which they talk to you for an hour before you sign documents? Do they meet with you once, and then you're stuck calling repeatedly, or left waiting for return calls? Be sure to ask, up front, how long the process takes. I tell you to ask these questions right away because it will help to set expectations on both sides. This trust is going to have a significant impact on your child.

Here are some tips to establish a good working relationship. Be kind to the attorney. If you want it done before you go on vacation, don't wait until a month before you leave to set an appointment. As an attorney, I'll tell you, that is NOT ok. We value the clients who value our time. If you have an initial meeting in the middle of December, don't expect your work to be done by the start of the year. Most attorneys have been in practice long enough that if you ask for an estimate, they will be able to give you a realistic one. When you make an appointment, keep it. Our personal and professional time is valuable.

Once your Supplemental Needs Trust is completed and you are informed that the drafting is done, make sure that the attorney takes the time to explain it to you. This doesn't mean a line-by-line read through, but you should be given an overview of the sections and why they are part of the document. Some sections of a Supplemental Needs Trust are based on statute and not every word in the document is written or crafted especially for you. This is because these sections are required by law.

When a trust is drafted by an attorney, there is often a document called a Certificate of Trust that is a short summary of the important information that a 3rd party may need to know. When I draft a Supplemental Needs Trust for a client, I always make sure that they have a document that I personally created, that tells them how to manage a Supplemental Needs Trust. It explains how to make sure that all funds are managed in accordance with the trust in a manner that won't disqualify the disabled person from future aid and assistance. A multiple page document that is basically written in a foreign language can be intimidating. You are paying for the documents, therefore you deserve to understand them and how to utilize them. There is nothing worse than paying a bunch of money for something and then leaving the office and thinking *now what?*

Once a Supplemental Needs Trust is drafted, there are next steps to take to "fund" the trust. If the trust is not funded properly, it will not work the way it was designed. No matter how good the attorney was that you hired, and no matter how much you paid, you still have to do work to make the Supplemental Needs Trust work for you.

The easiest way to fund a trust is to create a trust account at the bank. Discuss with your attorney which additional assets should be put into the trust. Let your accountant and financial advisor know that you have Supplemental Needs Trust.

Chapter 11

ABLE

Dear reader, I'm going to share a bonus with you. I am going to take you a step beyond the Supplemental Needs Trust and introduce you to the ABLE account. You will soon see that the play between the Supplemental Needs Trust and ABLE account is a beautiful thing.

First some background. President Obama singed the Achieving a Better Life Experience Act in late 2014. This created a financial instrument called an ABLE account. The goal of the ABLE account is to allow individuals with disabilities the opportunity to save money without getting disqualified from public benefits like Social Security or Medicaid.

Not just anyone with a disability can open an ABLE account. You or your disabled family member needs to meet certain criteria to qualify:

- Your disability was present before the age of 26; and
    - You are eligible for SSI or SSDI because of a disability
    - You experience blindness as determined by the Social Security Act; OR
    - You have a similarly severe disability with a written diagnosis from a licensed physician that can be produced if requested.

You must also certify that you have one of the following:

- Blindness as defined by the Social Security Act (SSA); OR

- A medically determinable physical or mental impairment with marked severed function limitation that has lasted, or is expected to last, at least 12 continuous months or result in death;

- AND you must have a written disability-related diagnosis signed by a physician.

Once you have determined qualification for the ABLE account, the next step is to research your options. Information about the Minnesota State plan can be found at:

https://savewithABLE.com/mn/home.html

However, just because you live in Minnesota doesn't mean that you need to choose the Minnesota ABLE plan. Other states administer their ABLE plans differently and most allow people from other states to join. Before making your selection, you should compare things such as minimum balance requirements, basic fees and any other fees, such as check fees or paper statement fees. Find the state program that best fits your needs and enroll in that state's plan if there is not a limitation on non-residents. The best way to do this is speak with your financial advisor. It is their job to help you compare and contrast investment options.

Now that you have opened an ABLE account, you can hide a bunch of money in it and still qualify for services and everything is wonderful, right? Wrong. There are limits to how much money can be put into the ABLE account each year. The limit is tied to the annual federal gift tax exclusion amount. In 2019 the amount is $15,000. There may also be account balance limits depending on whether the beneficiary is on Social Security.

So now that the money is in the ABLE account, how does one get it out? What is the benefit to this type of account? Like a 529 college savings plan, a 529A (ABLE) account allows the income to grow and not be taxed if spent on qualified disability expenses. According to savewithABLE.com, some examples of qualified disability expenses in the Minnesota plan are:

Education

- Tuition, Books, Supplies

Health & Wellness

- Therapy, Rehab, Medical Equipment

Housing

- Rent, Mortgage, Taxes, Heat, Water, Sewer, Etc.

Employment Training & Support

- Moving, On the Job Training

Transportation

- Purchase and/or modification of a vehicle, Mass Transit

Legal Fees

- Lawyer who Creates a Supplemental Needs Trust

Financial management

- Investment Advisor to help select ABLE account

Assistive Technology

- Durable Equipment, Adaptive Equipment

Personal Support Services

- Tracker, Smart Phone

Oversight & Monitoring

- Security, Monitoring, Oversight Services

Funeral and Burial

- Prepaid Expenses.

Chapter 12

Finale

TA-DA!! There you have it! I have revealed the secret. Did you catch it? Look closely at the diagram at the end of chapter 11. A 529 ABLE account can be used to pay for housing without affecting social security benefits. Allow me to spell this out:

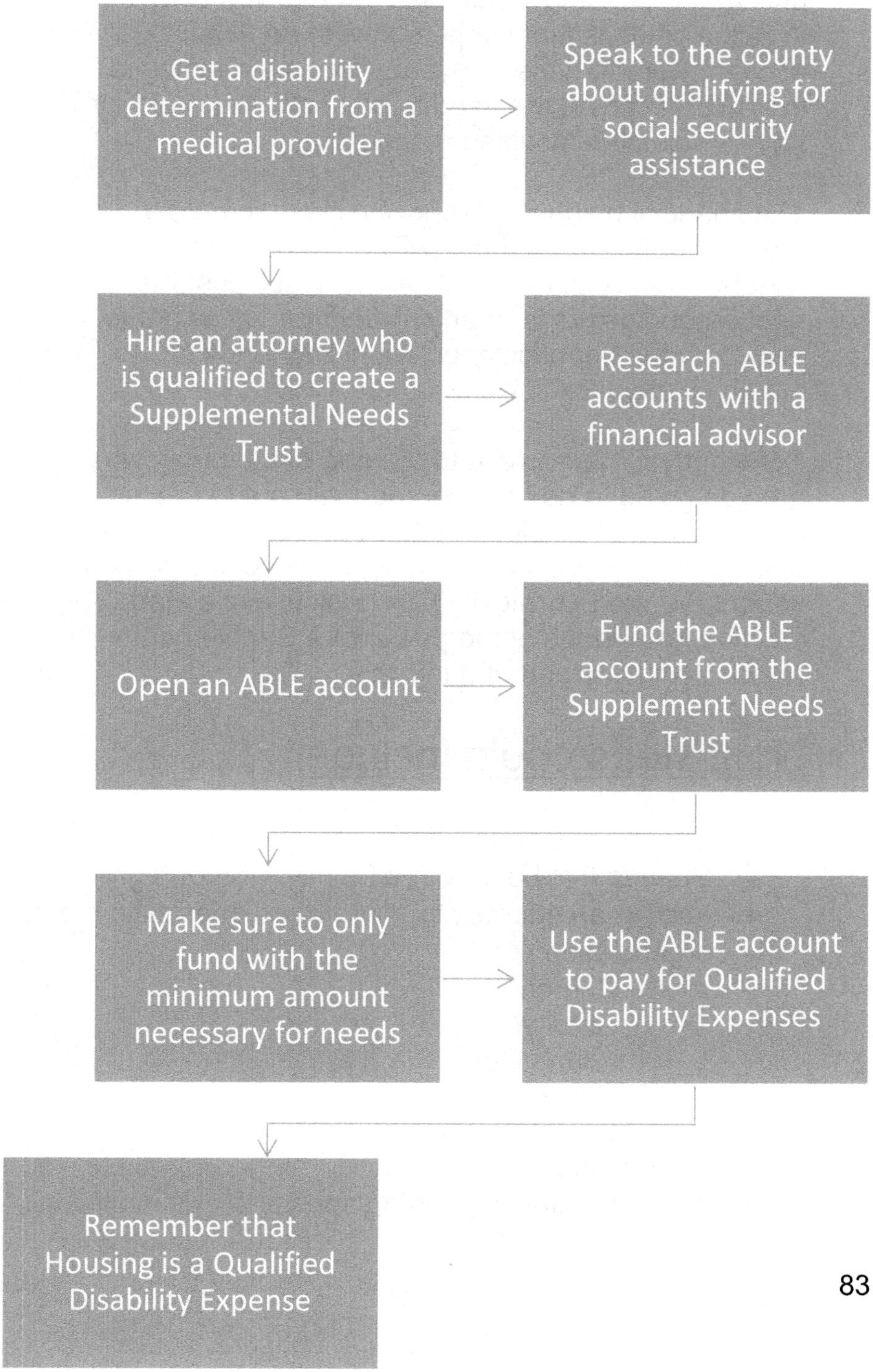
Get a disability determination from a medical provider
Speak to the county about qualifying for social security assistance
Hire an attorney who is qualified to create a Supplemental Needs Trust
Research ABLE accounts with a financial advisor
Open an ABLE account
Fund the ABLE account from the Supplement Needs Trust
Make sure to only fund with the minimum amount necessary for needs
Use the ABLE account to pay for Qualified Disability Expenses
Remember that Housing is a Qualified Disability Expense

You may have caught that I said minimum amount until further funding is necessary. Why, you ask? Well the catch is that if a person with an ABLE account were to pass away, any funds remaining in the ABLE account are used to pay back Medicaid for any services the disabled received.

The financial planners I work with like to create a method to "trickle-fund" the ABLE account from assets in the Supplemental Needs Trust. Just the right amount is put in at any given time, so as not to disqualify the beneficiary or risk losing funds to Medicaid payback.

Now that you have come to the end of the book, what are you going to do? I encourage you not to put the book on a shelf and let it gather dust. Remember, you didn't pick up this book because of the cover art. You sought the wisdom within. This book is just a start. Gaining knowledge of the power of a Supplemental Needs Trust is a part of a journey.

Next steps could include:

- Sharing this book with family
- Sharing this book with a friend or support group.
- Inviting an attorney to share more information to an organization.
    - Church
    - Charity
    - Foundation
    - Non-Profit
    - Social Group
    - Club
    - Groups supporting special needs individuals

The next steps should include:

- Meeting with an attorney, such as myself, who specializes in Supplemental Needs Trusts.

About the Author

I graduated Minnesota State University, Mankato with a double Business Management Major at the age of 20. In my third and final year of Hamline Law School, I won a CALI award and was introduced to the world of estate planning. I found my calling. I understood the world of wills and trusts and I was good at it.

Kiecker Law Office, LLC first opened for business in 2006. In 2009, when my first son was born, I took time off to be a parent. That is, and always will be, my favorite "job."

Today, in addition to the practice of law, I serve on the Board of Directors for Hope Rooted, a non-profit organization that supports Functional Medicine. Functional Medicine is patient-centered medical healing that looks at the whole person rather than simply treating symptoms. Functional medicine doctors work closely with patients to discover the underlying root cause or causes of their illness.

I am also on the Minnesota State University Alumni Association Board of Directors. Our mission is to engage alumni, friends and students in ways that benefit its members and Minnesota State University, Mankato through opportunities that stimulate a lifetime of interest, loyalty and support.

I now have 3 children and still run my own law firm. I do this partly because my oldest son is disabled. He has autism and ADHD. He is a flight risk and is considered vulnerable to social predators.

I know the material in this book because I live it. I understand special needs because I, too, have navigated the world of state and county forms. I am on a first name basis with my support planner and have gone through two different fiscal entities. I don't just create trusts for those who have disabled loved ones. I create a plan that will allow everyone to thrive and help the special needs individual survive.

Contact Me to Learn More

Omni N. Kiecker, Esq.
Kiecker Law Office, LLC
Metro: 952-843-8545
Greater MN: 507-609-2050
omni@kieckerlaw.com
www.kieckerlaw.com

Made in the USA
Monee, IL
04 November 2026

67380032R00049